HRYA

D0810532

Science Concepts SECOND SERIES

Adaptation

Alvin Silverstein, Virginia Silverstein,
and Laura Silverstein Nunn

Twenty-First Century Books
Minneapolis

Twenty-First Century Books
A division of Lerner Publishing Group, Inc.
241 First Avenue North
Minneapolis, MN 55401 U.S.A.

Website address: www.lernerbooks.com

Library of Congress Cataloging-in-Publication Data

Silverstein, Alvin.
    Adaptation / by Alvin Silverstein, Virginia Silverstein, and Laura Silverstein Nunn.
        p.   cm. — (Science concepts)
    Includes bibliographical references and index.
    ISBN 978-0-8225-3434-1 (lib. bdg. : alk. paper)
    1. Adaptation (Biology)—Juvenile literature. I. Silverstein, Virginia B. II. Nunn, Laura Silverstein. III. Title.
    QH546.S57 2008
    578.4—dc22   2007002862

Manufactured in the United States of America
1 2 3 4 5 6 – DP – 13 12 11 10 09 08

Contents

chapter one

Fit for Life

You can find living things in almost every part of the world—from the hot, rainy tropics to the icy polar regions to the dry deserts. They even live at the bottom of the ocean, where there is no light and the water is extremely cold.

Earth's living things (organisms) seem so different and varied. But they actually have something very important in common. They all seem to be perfectly suited to the places where they live (their habitats). Polar bears, for example, have white fur that helps them blend with the arctic snow and ice. Their heavy fur and the thick fat layer under their skin help keep them warm in their frigid home.

You might wonder how anything could survive in a desert. But many organisms can live there because their bodies are suited to dry weather. Most plants and animals need plenty of water to survive. But cactus plants can go for months without rain because they store water in their thick stems. And kangaroo rats, unlike most other animals, don't need to drink water at all. They get all the moisture they need from the seeds they eat.

The ancestors of cacti and kangaroo rats did not start out so well suited to dry conditions. Over many

Adaptation

Polar bears have adapted to life in the cold, icy Arctic.

generations, these species adapted, or changed to meet the demands of their environment. So did species that lived in other places. Over millions of years, the Earth's land, water, and weather have also changed many times. Living things have slowly adapted to the changing Earth. These adaptations have resulted in the many different kinds of plants, animals, and other creatures that live on our planet.

Scientists say that adaptation is an incredibly slow process. An adaptation is the result of gradual changes to a whole population of one kind of living thing, over

Did You Know?

No single organism can live everywhere on Earth. A polar bear, for example, would never survive in the jungle. An African elephant couldn't handle living in the Arctic. Most organisms live in the same environments their ancestors lived in thousands of years ago.

thousands of generations. Each small change helps the new generation survive a little better in the struggle for life.

Changing Environments

Is your neighborhood exactly like it was twenty years ago? Probably not. If you stay long enough in any environment, you're bound to see it change. Chances are, your parents or grandparents have seen lots of changes in their neighborhood over the years. Perhaps builders have cut down nearby trees to make room for new homes. New families have probably moved in, and others have moved out. The people who live in the neighborhood may change their behavior too, to fit the demands of new conditions and new neighbors.

People make changes and adjustments in their lives every single day. So do all other living things. Each organism has a special role in its habitat, and its adaptations help it perform this role and fit into its community of life. Scientists call an organism's role in its community a niche.

Think about your own neighborhood. There's a whole community of life right there. Let's say you live in the suburbs, in a home with a lawn. What good is the weedy crabgrass in your lawn? It may crowd out the grass, but it provides food for the local cottontail rabbits. And what about the rabbits? They're cute, but they don't eat enough crabgrass to

One of the lion's roles in its community is to control the zebra population.

keep your lawn looking nice, and they keep eating the plants in your vegetable garden. The rabbits are food for the foxes living in the woods at the end of your street. What's the foxes' niche? They control the neighborhood rabbit, mouse, and squirrel populations. Thanks to the foxes, you don't have mice in your basement or squirrels in your attic, and your garden has a few veggies left for you to eat.

Adaptation is essential for survival, especially when a habitat changes. For example, what if builders cut down the woods in your neighborhood? What happens to the foxes, the rabbits, the crabgrass, and all the other neighborhood organisms? When a habitat changes, the organisms living in it must adapt to the new conditions. They need to develop new ways to get food and shelter; escape danger; defend themselves and their young; and survive storms, drought, heat, and cold. Organisms that can't adapt or move away to a more suitable environment die. If changes are too dramatic or too widespread, all the organisms of a particular species, or kind, may die off. (The species may become extinct.)

Adapting to the World

How do organisms adapt to their habitats? One way is by changing their behavior. Various animals, including seals, monarch butterflies, and many birds, adapt to the changing seasons by migrating. As winter approaches and their summer habitats grow colder, these animals head for warmer places where there is plenty of food. Some animals travel thousands of miles each year. Other animals survive winter by hibernating. They fatten up or store food and then go into a kind of deep sleep. Their body processes slow down to conserve energy. They don't move, and they breathe very slowly. Plants can't travel or move away like animals can, but they may become dormant (temporarily stop growing and developing).

Another way organisms adapt to their habitats is by developing physical traits that help them survive. A woodpecker, for example, constantly hammers its beak against tree trunks to find food, communicate, and make a nest. Its powerful neck muscles help it hammer hard and fast. The hammering doesn't hurt its head because its skull is thick and spongy. Its strong beak has a sharp tip that cuts into the wood.

> ### Did You Know?
> Arctic terns make the longest migrations. These birds fly as far as 20,000 miles (32,187 kilometers) each year, from their home in the Arctic to the other end of the world in the Antarctic and back again!

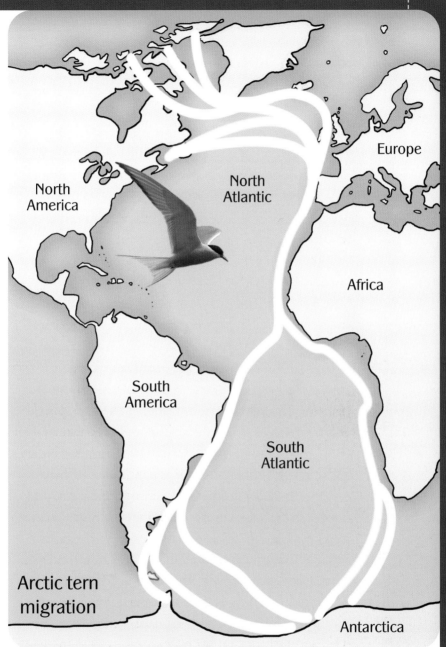

The arctic tern is the world's champion migrator. It flies from the Arctic to the Antarctic, then back to the Arctic, each year.

The woodpecker's sturdy legs and stiff tail feathers steady it on the tree trunk. It uses its long, barbed tongue to pull insects out of the cracks it makes.

Adapting to Each Other

Adapting to a habitat is about more than just the habitat's physical conditions (such as heat and cold or freshwater and salt water). Living things must also adapt to other organisms in their habitat. Many of these adaptations involve ways of getting food and avoiding predators. The woodpecker's specialized head, beak, and tongue, for example, are adaptations that help it catch insects living under tree bark. The kangaroo rat's cheek pouches allow it to gather seeds from plants scattered over large areas without having to return to its burrow very often. And its strong legs help it leap away from hungry foxes and snakes. Many animals and plants produce poisons to protect them from creatures that might eat them.

The woodpecker's entire body is well adapted to hammering against tree trunks.

Poisonous organisms often have bright colors and vivid markings to warn away attackers.

Some organisms survive by teaming up with other organisms. Crocodiles, rhinos, buffalos, and some other large animals get rid of pests, such as ticks, with the help of little birds. The birds eat the pests and get food as they help their partners stay healthy. Some plants, such as the acacia, have ants as bodyguards to protect them from animals that eat acacia leaves. The ants bite the noses of munching animals, annoying them so much that they go away. In return, the acacia gives the ants food and shelter. The ants live in the plant's thorns and drink its sweet nectar.

The following chapters take a closer look at how different adaptations help organisms survive in their habitats.

chapter two

Adaptation and Evolution

Our world is constantly changing. In fact, most scientists believe Earth has been continually changing for billions of years, and that its organisms have been changing to adapt to the planet's changes. This process is called evolution. The theory of evolution explains how Earth and all its living things formed and developed, generation after generation, from the beginning of life on Earth to the present. Scientists have collected a great deal of evidence to support this theory.

According to the theory of evolution, life first appeared about three or four billion years ago, after Earth's crust had formed and cooled. The first living things were very simple—just microscopic blobs of chemicals. As time passed and Earth changed, these simple organisms evolved (changed and developed) into more complex organisms that were better suited to their environment. Different groups of organisms became specialized in different ways, adapting not only to the conditions on Earth but also to each other. Some of the new organisms could make their own food; some got energy and building materials by eating other organisms. They passed their specialized traits to new generations, which evolved into an ever greater variety of forms. Evolution eventually produced all the different species that have lived on Earth.

Evolution is not a thing of the past, as many people believe. Organisms keep adapting slowly to their changing environments. Adaptation is an important part of evolution. But how exactly do living things adapt? Do they sense environmental change and alter their bodies or behaviors in response? No, organisms don't direct the process of adaptation and evolution. But no one could figure out how the process works until a young Englishman took a trip around the world in the 1830s.

Charles Darwin set sail on a five-year scientific expedition in 1831.

Darwin's Journey

At age twenty-two, Charles Darwin accepted an exciting job offer: naturalist for a five-year scientific expedition on a ship called the *Beagle*. The *Beagle* left Plymouth, England, in 1831 and sailed south along the west coast of Europe and Africa. Then it crossed the Atlantic Ocean to Brazil and spent more than a year traveling around South America. Sailing west across the Pacific Ocean, the *Beagle* completed a circle around the world by way of New Zealand, Australia,

Evolution in Action

Before the 1800s, the evolution of life on Earth was very gradual. Generally, people could not observe biological adaptation in a short period of time. But in the 1800s, the environment started to change at a much faster rate. The human population began to grow very quickly, and people began using machinery to do a lot of their work. This industrial revolution drastically changed or destroyed many organisms' natural habitats. These fast-changing habitats led to some surprising adaptations.

The peppered moth is one species that adapted rapidly to environmental changes. Before the industrial revolution, most of the peppered moths that lived in Great Britain were white with black spots. A small number of them were completely black. The light-colored moths blended with the bark of the trees they rested on during the day, but the

the southern tip of Africa, and finally back to Brazil, before heading home to England in 1836. This route gave Darwin a chance to study plants, animals, fossils, and geological formations that no European naturalist had explored before. He collected and classified many samples of plants and

black ones were easily visible to birds, which ate them. The black moths were less likely to survive long enough to reproduce, keeping their numbers small.

During the mid-1800s, however, soot from the many new factories in Great Britain started to blacken the bark of trees. The light-colored moths now stood out more than the black ones. Birds ate mainly light-colored moths, and their numbers dropped sharply. The black moths, on the other hand, now had an advantage. Birds were less likely to spot them against the sooty trees. The black moths quickly multiplied and became more common than the light-colored type.

When Great Britain passed clean air laws in the 1970s, air pollution decreased. As tree trunks became less sooty, the moth population began to change again. Light-colored moths multiplied, and black ones became less common.

Darwin sailed around the world on this ship, the Beagle. *The plants and animals he saw on his voyage helped him form his ideas about evolution.*

animals from both coastal and inland areas. He also wrote detailed notes in his journal.

One of the *Beagle*'s stops was the Galápagos Islands, about 600 miles (966 km) off the coast of Ecuador. These islands had been created by volcanic eruptions long after the continents had formed. The organisms living there had come from the mainland, carried either by winds or by ocean currents. Darwin was amazed by the diversity of species on the islands compared to those in Europe. He saw animal species on the Galápagos Islands that no one had found anywhere else on Earth.

Among the various organisms Darwin studied were several species of finches, small birds that were very common on the islands. When he got back to

England, Darwin realized that the Galápagos finch species were closely related to one another and to a finch species he had found on the west coast of South America. All these finches looked similar, but each species had unique physical traits that reflected its specialized eating habits. For example, the shape of the beak depended on whether the finches ate seeds and cacti on the ground or berries and insects in trees.

Darwin reasoned that all the different finches on the islands were descendants of the mainland species. He thought the finches had adapted to the different kinds of food available on the various islands where they settled. In each generation, birds were born with slightly different-shaped beaks. Some variations were better suited to eating certain

These sketches show four different types of finches that Charles Darwin found on the Galápagos Islands. Each bird was specially adapted to the environment in which it lived.

foods. The well-fed birds were healthier, stronger, and had more babies. It seemed as though nature was selecting a particular type of finch for each niche in the island communities. Over many generations, specialized populations of finches developed, and eventually they became separate species.

In 1859 Darwin introduced his theory of evolution in the book *The Origin of Species*. In this book, Darwin suggests that organisms that happen to be better suited to the world's ever-changing habitats are more likely to survive and reproduce than organisms that are less suited to their habitats. This process is called natural selection, or "survival of the fittest."

According to Darwin's theory:

1. Individual organisms tend to produce more offspring than their environment can support. All members of a species' population in a particular habitat must compete for the available resources. There is a struggle for survival.

2. Members of the same species have variations in their traits. Nature "selects" traits that already exist in the population. Individuals whose traits are best suited to their habitat are most likely to survive and reproduce.

3. The surviving organisms pass on their favorable traits to their offspring. Over time, habitats change and make different traits favorable. As nature selects new traits, the population begins to differ from the original population. Eventually the organisms become so different from the original individuals that the population develops into a new species.

What Is a Species?

The term *species* is Latin for "appearance" or "kind." Originally scientists identified species by their appearance, since members of a species usually look similar. However, some different species, such as the African elephant and the Indian elephant, look very similar. Modern scientists use many kinds of evidence to classify species. They look at an organism's internal structure, what it eats, and how it reproduces. The chemicals in the organism's cells also provide important clues.

Members of a species can breed with other members of the same species and produce healthy offspring. Usually they cannot do this with members of another species. Dogs and cats, for example, cannot mate and produce little cogs and dats. A donkey and a horse *can* mate and produce offspring called mules. But mules cannot produce offspring of their own.

What Causes Variation?

If you look at photos of your family, you'll probably notice that you, your parents, your brothers and sisters, your cousins, and your other blood relatives look rather similar. Maybe many of you have the same color hair, the same nose shape, or the same smile. You'll probably see differences in the photos too. Perhaps your uncle is much taller than your father, or maybe your eyes are a different color from those of your brothers or sisters.

These dogs may look very different, but they all belong to the same species.

Heredity (passing traits from parent to offspring) determines these similarities and differences.

Your family photos illustrate Darwin's idea that members of the same species have variations in their traits. Just like humans, other species have varying traits too. Think about the physical variations among dogs. Chihuahuas, poodles, bulldogs, and Great Danes all belong to the same species, but their bodies are very different.

Although Darwin realized how important heredity and variation are in evolution, he didn't know how heredity works or why variation happens. An Austrian monk, teacher, and scientist named Gregor Mendel began to solve that mystery in 1865, but no one paid attention to him until 1900. And it would take another fifty years for scientists to figure out the entire process.

Each organism has a complete set of instructions inside each of its body cells. This "owner's manual" covers everything each cell needs to do in order to live. Parents pass these instructions on to their offspring when they reproduce. These instructions are written in code in a chemical called DNA (deoxyribonucleic acid). DNA is made up of units called genes. Together, the genes determine all of an organism's hereditary traits. Normally cells multiply by copying their DNA and then dividing in half. When a cell divides, each new "daughter cell" gets a complete set of DNA—all the genes of its parent cell.

Copying DNA

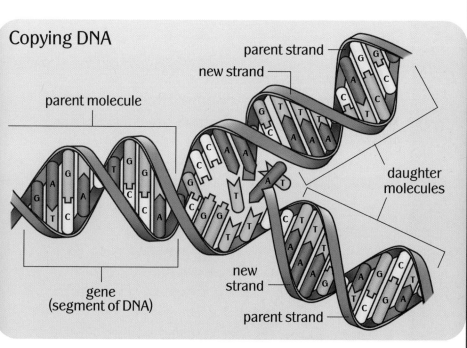

parent strand

new strand

parent molecule

daughter molecules

gene
(segment of DNA)

new strand

parent strand

Before a cell divides to form two cells, it copies its DNA. This chemical contains all of the cell's hereditary information, written in a four-letter code. Each new cell gets a complete set of DNA.

When cells divide, variation can happen in two ways. First, errors in copying may produce daughter DNA that is slightly different from the parent DNA. Such changes in DNA are called mutations. Most mutations are neither helpful nor harmful. Some produce traits that make an organism less fit to survive. A few result in traits that actually help survival. Mutations can pass from parent to offspring during reproduction. As generations go by, the number of individuals with a certain mutation may grow. Later, if living conditions change, mutations that did not seem to be helpful may turn out to be very important. Organisms carrying such changes in their genes may have just the new abilities they need to survive better than others of their species.

Variation can also appear when organisms reproduce sexually. In sexual reproduction, cells divide in a special way to produce sex cells. Most body cells contain complete sets of DNA with two copies of each kind of gene, but sex cells contain only half sets of DNA. (They have only one copy of each kind of gene.) A male sex cell and a female sex cell join to create a new organism. The offspring gets one gene of each kind from the male and one gene of each kind from the female. The two genes in a particular pair may be quite different. For example, the offspring may get a gene for blue eye color from one parent and a gene for brown eye color from the other. Heredity in sexual reproduction is like dealing a new hand from a well-shuffled deck of cards. Each

How Did the Giraffe Get Its Long Neck?

Scientists once believed that giraffes got their long necks by stretching to reach leaves high up in trees. Darwin's theory of evolution offers a different explanation: Giraffes normally vary in height, just as people do. The length of their necks varies too. The ancient ancestors of today's giraffes had necks not much longer than those of horses or antelopes. But some of these prehistoric giraffes happened to have necks a little longer than the average. The longer-necked giraffes could reach leaves higher up in trees than the shorter-necked giraffes could. When food was scarce, the long-necked giraffes got more to eat. They were healthier, stronger, and more likely to survive and reproduce. Many of their offspring inherited the genes for long necks from their parents. Gradually, as variations in neck length continued to appear, the surviving giraffes had necks that were longer and longer.

offspring gets a complete set of gene pairs, but chance determines which gene in each pair comes from which parent.

In each pair of genes, one may be dominant. The variation of the trait that it produces will always appear, no matter what kind of gene is paired with it. The other gene in the pair may be recessive. The variation it produces will not show unless the offspring happens to receive two of that particular gene. For example, the gene for brown eyes is dominant, and the gene for blue eyes is recessive. A person with brown eyes may have two brown-eye genes, or one brown and one blue. But someone with blue eyes has two blue-eye genes. A recessive trait can appear only when a person has two of the genes for it. (The inheritance of eye color is actually somewhat more complicated. Other pairs of genes are also involved. That is why people can have not only brown or blue eyes but also various shades of gray, green, and hazel eyes. And in rare cases, two blue-eyed parents may have children with brown eyes.)

How Life Has Evolved

Scientists believe that the first living things appeared on Earth three or four billion years ago. These first organisms were very simple, each consisting of just one cell. They lived in the oceans that covered much of the planet. They took in raw materials from the water and made their own food by chemical reactions.

Gradually, over many millions of years, mutations appeared. Some of them made the simple organisms a little better able to survive. Some organisms began to get their food by eating other living things. Some single cells combined to form groups of cells, which stayed together. These were the first multicellular organisms. Gradually their different cells became specialized for different jobs, such as getting food, sensing light or warmth, escaping from danger, and reproducing. Cell structures changed, too. Eventually some organisms developed into plants that could make their own food

Sequence of Life Forms

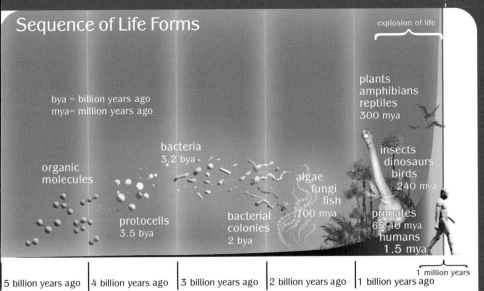

explosion of life

bya = billion years ago
mya= million years ago

plants
amphibians
reptiles
300 mya

organic
molecules

bacteria
3.2 bya

algae
fungi
fish
700 mya

insects
dinosaurs
birds
240 mya

protocells
3.5 bya

bacterial
colonies
2 bya

primates
65–40 mya
humans
1.5 mya

1 million years

| 5 billion years ago | 4 billion years ago | 3 billion years ago | 2 billion years ago | 1 billion years ago |

At first, Earth's organisms were very simple. Over billions of years, Earth's living things have become more varied and complex.

by photosynthesis (using the energy from sunlight to make glucose, a kind of sugar, from water and carbon dioxide).

Some of the early organisms developed into animals, which could not make their own food. Some animals ate plants, some ate other animals, and some ate waste and bits of dead matter from plants and animals. Some of the early animals developed hard outer shells that helped protect them from predators. These outer shells also anchored the muscles that helped the animals move. More millions of years went by, and natural variations led to the development of vertebrates. A vertebrate is an animal with a skeleton (including a backbone) inside its body. Vertebrates had a big advantage over invertebrates (animals without backbones). The vertebrates were lighter and faster, which helped them catch food and escape from their enemies.

The early plants and animals multiplied and spread out through the oceans. They also entered the rivers and streams that ran through Earth's lands. Until about 425 million years ago, organisms lived only in the water. Then plants began to invade the land, adapting to the new conditions there. Some of these new plants could grow roots down into the earth. Roots helped them stay put and take in water and other chemicals from the rocks. Some plants also developed leaves that could spread outward and upward to catch more sunlight.

As plants became established on land, animals followed to eat this new food source. The first animals to invade the land were invertebrates, such as insects and spiders. They were so small and light that wind could carry them over long distances. These first land animals needed adaptations to survive and thrive in their new environment. They couldn't breathe with gills because gills work only underwater. But natural variation had produced some insects and spiders that could take in air directly from the atmosphere. Land animals also developed stronger muscles to support their bodies out of the water.

Meanwhile, vertebrates in oceans and streams became more plentiful and varied. They were all fish. The first fish were jawless creatures that ate by sucking up bits of dead matter. Then fish with jaws and stronger skeletons developed. Their adaptations allowed them to swim faster and eat other fish. Some

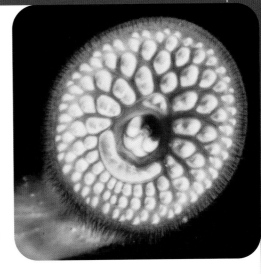

The sea lamprey is a modern jawless fish. It attaches to other fish with its round, tooth-filled mouth and sucks out their blood and other body fluids.

of their descendants were the first vertebrates to invade the land, about four hundred million years ago.

Jaws!

What's the first thing you imagine when you hear the word *jaws*? Thanks to the classic horror movie *Jaws*, it's probably sharks. Their huge mouths contain several rows of teeth. New teeth grow in a row nearest the inside of a shark's mouth. The inner rows move outward as the skin grows outward, like a conveyor belt, to replace the outer teeth that fall out. Some sharks can lose as many as thirty thousand teeth in a lifetime.

The shark's jaws gave it an important advantage over jawless fish, which couldn't catch and eat living prey. But sharks' skeletons are still rather primitive; they are made of soft cartilage. Fish species that developed later had hard, bony skeletons, which provided better support for their muscles. Eventually, this new feature helped their descendants adapt to life on land.

Around the time fish developed jaws and bony skeletons, natural variation produced other interesting structures: longer, stronger fins and lungs that could get oxygen directly from the air. These variations weren't of much use to water animals. But when their watery habitat changed, the variations became very useful indeed. Imagine this: Four hundred million years ago, a primitive lungfish was living in a pond somewhere on Earth. For a few minutes each day it flopped along the muddy shore, then slipped back into the warm water. This exercise helped strengthen its fins. Then the weather turned very hot, and it didn't rain for a long time. The pond started to dry up. As the pond shrank, the animals living in it got more and more crowded. Some of them died. But not the lungfish. It flipped and flopped its way out of the pond and across the land until it happened to find a bigger pond.

There are modern fish very much like that primitive lungfish. The walking catfish, for example, lives in ponds and can travel overland to a new home if its old one dries up. But some of the lungfish's descendants developed variations that made them even better suited to life on land. They evolved into amphibians, animals that can live both in the water and on land. Today's frogs and toads, for example, breathe air using lungs and walk (or hop) on land with legs that developed from the fish's fins. Many adult amphibians spend most of their time on land but do not usually travel far from the water. They return to the water to mate and lay their eggs.

The bodies of tadpoles, which live in water, change drastically as they become frogs, which can live on land.

Like amphibians, reptiles, birds, and mammals also evolved from those first land vertebrates. They developed many new features that helped them survive on land. These adaptations included tougher skin that could stay healthy when it was dry, stronger leg muscles, and stronger hearts and lungs. Over time, adaptation produced many different kinds of land animals, which could live in a great variety of habitats. For example, some animals living in cold regions developed into species able to stand colder weather. Some animals living in deserts developed into species that could survive long periods of drought. Some animals living in the mountains developed into species that could live in the thinner atmosphere at high altitudes.

Gradually living things spread over all the lands of the Earth, each kind adapted to its particular habitat and filling a niche in that habitat's community of life. Scientists call this

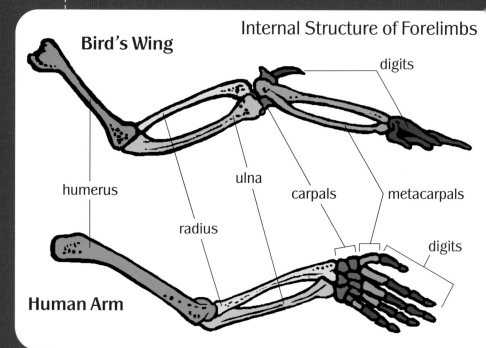

Internal Structure of Forelimbs

Bird's Wing

digits

humerus

ulna

carpals

metacarpals

radius

digits

Human Arm

A bird's wing and a human arm look different and work differently, but they have the same bone structure inside them.

process adaptive radiation, or divergent evolution. It happens when two or more species evolve from a common ancestor and then become increasingly different over time. We can see evidence of divergent evolution when we compare the structures of different kinds of animals. For example, let's examine the forelimbs of many different vertebrates:

• The front legs of an alligator are relatively short and weak. It can run only short distances; usually it crawls along, dragging its belly on the ground. Like the rest of its body, the alligator's legs are covered with tough, scaly skin. Three of its five toes on each front leg end in sharp claws.

The forelimbs of alligators (top right), cats (above), *and* humans (bottom right) *have evolved very differently over time.*

• A cat's front legs have toes with sharp claws, too—five of them. A cat's legs are much longer in proportion to its body than an alligator's legs are, and they're strong enough for running and leaping. A cat can use its front paws to hit or grab things, but when it wants to carry something, it uses its mouth.

• The "front legs" of a human being are called arms, because we don't use them for walking or running. Our

The forelimbs of horses (above), *dolphins* (top left), *and birds* (bottom left) *also show divergent evolution.*

five-fingered hands have flat fingernails to protect the fingertips, and our thumbs can curl around to meet the other fingers in a strong or delicate grip. We use our arms for holding and carrying things, for eating, and for making and using tools.

• A horse's long, strong front legs each end in a single toe covered by a tough hoof. A horse's legs are suited for running swiftly. Its hooves cushion and protect its toes when they slam on the ground.

• A bird's front legs have evolved into wings with no fingers or toes. Birds can't use their wings for walking or holding things. But wings are perfect for gliding and flying through the air. Strong chest and wing muscles and very light bones are adaptations for flight, and so are feathers. Feathers provide a light, warm covering and help a bird lift into the air and steer its flight.

• The front legs of a dolphin are flippers that look like a fish's fins. Flippers are adaptations for swimming. The dolphin's ancestors were four-legged land animals that re-adapted to life in the water.

These animals' forelimbs look different and work differently, but X-rays show they all have the same basic bone structure. A single heavy bone in the upper part of the limb is joined at the "elbow" to two slimmer bones. These in turn join with some wrist bones that look like pebbles fitted tightly together. The wrist bones lead to a series of finger bones. Over time, the finger bones of different vertebrates evolved to better suit the animals' changing ways of life. In some species, fingers disappeared. In others, fingers combined into one or more stronger supports.

These forelimbs are examples of homology. Homologous body parts have the same basic structure, but they have evolved into very different forms, often for different uses. Homology appears in the course of adaptive radiation, as organisms adapt to different conditions or ways of life.

Evolution can also result in analogous structures. These are body parts in different species that look similar and serve similar needs but differ in their structure. Analogous body parts evolved in different ways from different ancestors.

Close Cousins

Scientists have discovered that "sea cows," or manatees, are closely related to elephants! These large mammals live in warm ocean waters from Florida to northern Brazil, and in rivers in western Africa and South America's Amazon basin. DNA evidence shows that an elephant-like ancestor of manatees adapted to life in the water, and its legs evolved into flippers.

Manatees (left) *and elephants* (right) *evolved from a common ancestor.*

Butterflies, birds, and bats developed wings in different ways from different ancestors.

Internal Structure of Wings

butterfly wing

bird wing

bat wing

Dolphins and sharks, for example, have similar body shapes. Their bodies are smoothly curved and streamlined, and they have flippers or fins and strong tails to help them move. These similarities are adaptations for swimming. That's why dolphins look more like sharks and other fish than like their four-footed mammal ancestors that lived on land.

Fish and sea mammals developed their analogous body shapes by a process called convergent evolution. In convergent evolution, distantly related species develop similar adaptations to their habitats as time goes by. Birds, bats, and butterflies provide another example of convergent evolution. These creatures all have wings, but they inherited their wings from different ancestors. Each ancestor independently developed this adaptation for flying, and the internal structures of the three wings are quite different.

Land before Time

Australia seems to be caught in a time warp. This island continent split off from the other lands of the Earth about one hundred million years ago. At that time, most mammals there were marsupials. Marsupials produce young that complete their development after birth, in a pouch on their mother's belly. Australia's other mammals were a few egg-laying species.

Meanwhile, most of the mammals in the rest of the world were placental mammals. These are animals whose young develop fully inside their mother's body, getting nourishment from an organ called a placenta. Over most of Earth's lands, placental mammals were more successful in the struggle for survival, and all the marsupials except opossums died out.

Australia's marsupials were cut off from the rest of the world. They evolved separately—and differently. Divergent evolution filled Australia's various habitats with a great variety of mammals. These new mammals were nearly all marsupials, because there were no placental mammals to compete with them. That's why there are so many marsupials in Australia and why kangaroos, koalas, and other Australian species don't live anywhere else in the world. It's also why Australia doesn't have many of the animals that live on other continents.

Australia's varied habitats are similar to habitats in other parts of the world. So convergent evolution occurred there too. Many Australian mammals are amazingly similar to placental mammals in the rest of the world. For example, there are marsupial "mice" and "cats" that look and act much like the mice and cats in Europe, Asia, and the Americas. The egg-laying echidnas of Australia, the aardvarks of Africa, and the anteaters of the tropical Americas are another example of this convergent evolution. Each of these species independently developed a long, tapered snout and a long tongue for probing into anthills.

chapter three

Extreme Habitats

Can you imagine a dolphin living in the Sahara desert? How about a polar bear living in the Amazon rain forest? Or a cactus plant in Antarctica? Could these organisms survive in these habitats? Of course not. Each living thing is specially adapted to a particular habitat—and in these imaginary cases, the organisms and their habitats are really mismatched.

A dolphin could never survive in the hot, dry Sahara. Its streamlined body and fins are perfect for swimming, but on the desert sand, the dolphin would not be able to hunt for food or escape from the hot sun or predators. A polar bear isn't suited to the steamy tropics, either. Its thick fur and the insulating fat beneath its skin would make it overheated in a hot climate. And a cactus plant couldn't live in Antarctica. Antarctica is bitter cold and covered with snow and ice. Some cacti make a kind of antifreeze that keeps the water stored in their stems from freezing in cold weather. But how would cacti get water? They have no way to melt snow, and it almost never rains in Antarctica.

There are many different kinds of habitats all over the world. Some of them are quite extreme—

very hot or cold, very dry or wet, and so on. It's hard to believe that anything could live in these extreme habitats. But organisms have developed adaptations that have made it possible for them to survive even in the harshest conditions.

Urban Animals

Many creatures have adapted successfully to the city, a habitat very different from the habitats of their ancestors. Some common city dwellers are the pigeon, blackbird, gray squirrel, mouse, rat, mosquito, housefly, cockroach, moth, spider, ant, beetle, and flea.

Desert Life

In most places on Earth, rain falls regularly throughout the year, with dry spells from time to time. But deserts are dry most of the time, with only a few rainfalls. (And when it rains, it pours!) Deserts typically get no more than 10 inches (25 centimeters) of rain every year. Desert plants have very short growing periods—usually right after a rainfall. After a rainfall, some plants produce colorful flowers. The flowers shrivel and fall off as the region dries up again.

Flowers bloom in the desert after a rare rainfall.

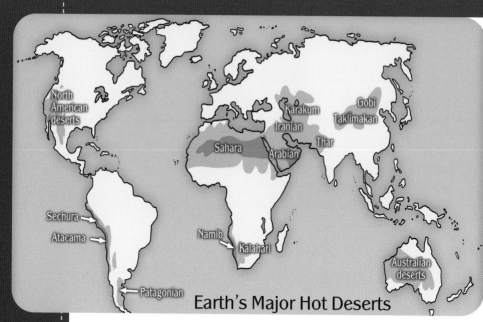

Earth's Major Hot Deserts

Five continents—North and South America, Africa, Asia, and Australia—contain major hot deserts. Europe contains a tiny hot desert (in Spain). All of Antarctica is a cold desert.

Where Are the Deserts?

Every continent in the world contains a desert. The world's largest hot desert is the Sahara, which covers 3.5 million square miles (more than 9 million square km) of northern Africa. The Namib and Kalahari deserts cover much of southern Africa. Other large deserts include the Arabian, Iranian, Karakum, and Gobi deserts in Asia. Ten deserts take up nearly 20 percent of Australia. Smaller deserts exist in the western United States and Mexico, western South America, and southeastern South America.

Deserts can get really hot in the daytime. In fact, daytime temperatures often go above 100°F (38°C). But nights can get cold, with temperatures dropping as low as 32°F (0°C) in the winter. Why do the temperatures drop so much at night? A desert has very little humidity (water vapor in the air) compared to other habitats. In a tropical rain forest, for example, the plentiful water vapor in the air absorbs sunlight during the day. At night the blanket of moist air traps heat inside the forest. But a desert has so little humidity and vegetation to hold in the heat that it cools down quickly after sunset. When the sun comes up, it doesn't take long for the desert to get scorching hot again.

A desert may not seem like an ideal habitat for plant life, but plants do live in deserts. In fact, plants have adapted to scanty rainfall in several ways. Some store large amounts of water in their leaves, roots, or stems. For example, the spongy tissue

Cold Deserts?

Not all deserts are hot. Some deserts, such as the Gobi in Asia, are very cold both day and night for most of the year. However, the Gobi desert does get hot on summer days—often 90° to 100°F (32° to 38°C) and sometimes as high as 113°F (45°C). On the desert continent of Antarctica, it is cold all year round. The cold deserts may get precipitation in the form of snow, but usually less than 10 inches (25 cm) per year.

The barrel cactus is a plant that has adapted to the desert's dry conditions.

inside the stem of a barrel cactus swells with water after a rainfall; the cactus gradually shrinks as it uses the water. The mesquite tree has a different adaptation: roots that can reach as deep as 263 feet (80 meters) underground! Other plants have adaptations that reduce water loss from their leaves, such as losing their leaves during dry periods or having very small leaves. Many desert plants have no leaves at all. Their large green stems carry out photosynthesis instead. (In most plants, photosynthesis takes place mainly in the leaves.)

Animals have adapted to desert life too. To avoid the daytime heat, most desert animals are nocturnal (active at night). Small desert animals spend their days in underground burrows, while large animals escape the hot sun by staying in the shade. Since water is scarce, desert animals drink very little or no water. They get most or all of the water they need from the food they eat.

When you picture a desert, a camel may be the first animal you imagine. Camels are well adapted to the desert's scarcity of food and water. A camel can go for three months without drinking water. When a camel eats, it stores fat in its hump. The camel can use its stored fat for energy when no food is available. The hump shrinks as the camel uses up the fat, and it grows when the camel eats again.

Three other adaptations help a camel deal with sand. Double rows of long eyelashes keep windblown sand out of a camel's eyes. A camel can close its nostrils to keep sand out of its nose. Its wide feet let it walk on sand without sinking.

Camels are well adapted to heat too. Many animals pant to stay cool, but they lose water from their bodies when they do this.

Wild camels live in the desert in China. Camels are well adapted to the desert's sand, heat, and scarce food and water.

A camel has to conserve water, so it copes with the desert heat differently. Its body temperature can safely vary throughout the day from 93°F to 107°F (34°C to 42°C). The camel's temperature rises during the day and falls during the night. Most mammals can't do this; they must keep their body temperature steady to stay healthy.

Most desert animals are much smaller than camels. Kangaroo rats, for example, are little rodents that are perfectly adapted to desert life. Kangaroo rats don't need to drink water. They get all the water their bodies need from the seeds they eat. Special adaptations also keep them from losing much water. For example, their urine is very concentrated. (It contains very little water.)

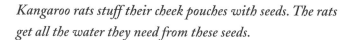

Kangaroo rats stuff their cheek pouches with seeds. The rats get all the water they need from these seeds.

Adaptation

Kangaroo rats beat the heat by sleeping through the hot, sunny days in their burrows, deep in the soil or sand. They plug up the entrances to keep their burrows cool and hold in moisture. They go out to gather seeds at night, when it's cooler. Kangaroo rats have short front legs with strong claws for digging burrows, but they don't use their front legs for walking or running. They get around by leaping with their long hind legs. (Although kangaroo rats are not related to kangaroos, the rats were named after kangaroos because both have long legs and leap in similar ways.) Hairy soles on their big hind feet help them move on loose, sandy soil.

Life in the Polar Regions

If you think desert life is harsh, imagine living near the North or South Pole. The polar regions are the coldest places on Earth. They are covered with snow and ice for much of the year. Only the tundra areas at the poles' outer edges experience a brief summer thaw. The winters are unbelievably cold, averaging about -22°F (-30°C) in the Arctic (northern polar region).

The polar regions are dark twenty-four hours a day during the winter. During the summer, they have continuous daylight.

The Good Life

Imagine living in a place where the weather never gets too hot or too cold—it stays about 80°F (27°C) all year long. There's plenty of water and lots of delicious food to eat. This habitat is not a fantasy; it's a tropical rain forest. Life is so good in tropical rain forests that two-thirds of the world's species live there. Rain forests are crowded with creatures that compete with each other for food and space.

Tropical rain forests are found near the equator in Asia, Africa, South America, Central America, and on many Pacific islands. Almost half of the world's rain forests are in South America. A lot of rain falls in the rain forest—usually at least 70 inches (178 cm) per year. Some rain forests get more than 200 inches (508 cm) of rain per year! The rest of the world gets an average of 36 inches (91 cm) of rain per year.

Tall, broad-leaved evergreen trees grow very close together in a tropical rain forest. The forest has four levels. Each one provides a different kind of habitat for a wide variety of organisms. The highest level is the emergent layer. It is made up of the tops of the tallest trees, which may grow as tall as 270 feet (82 m). Various insects live up there, along with birds such as the scarlet macaw. Most of a rain forest's species live in the canopy, the next level down. In the canopy, the trees' leaves and branches form an umbrella-like covering over the forest. This level is very high off the ground, too—100 to 200 feet (30 to 61 m) from the forest floor.

The third level of the forest is the understory. This level is made up of small trees, vines, and palms, as well as shrubs and ferns. Snakes, lizards, insects such as beetles and bees, and small mammals such as the kinkajou live here. Bigger mammals such as jaguars may spend time on large tree branches, looking for prey down below. The shade provided by the canopy makes the understory dark and cool. The lowest level of the rain forest is the forest floor, where herbs, mosses, and fungi grow. The many animals that live at ground level range from ants to elephants.

The coldest temperature recorded on Earth occurred in the Antarctic (southern polar region). It was -128.6°F (-89.2°C). Even in the summer, Antarctic temperatures rarely get above freezing. But summers in parts of the Arctic are warmer, with an average temperature of 50°F (10°C).

Antarctica is an ice-covered continent that covers more than 5.4 million square miles (14 million square km). It is larger than the United States, and sheets of ice surround it. The continent has mountains, valleys, and glaciers. It doesn't get much snowfall because the temperatures are too cold. Only a few plants, such as mosses, can survive in Antarctica. A few insects and other tiny creatures can also survive the harsh conditions of the mainland. But most Antarctic animals live on the edges of the continent, in and near the ocean. They include various fish, shrimplike krill, seals, whales, penguins, and other seabirds.

Penguins are the best known Antarctic animals. These birds can't fly in the air at all, but they can "fly" very well in the water. Their wings have adapted into strong flippers that propel them through the water. Their streamlined bodies let

Did You Know?
The largest animals that live all year long on the mainland of Antarctica are tiny wingless insects called springtails. These creatures are less than 0.2 inch (0.5 cm) long!

Emperor penguins can swim quickly through the cold waters around Antarctica.

them glide with little resistance. A penguin's body is specially adapted to surviving in icy waters. A thick, waterproof layer of outer feathers covers an inner layer of soft, fluffy feathers. The two layers of feathers trap air to help the penguin float and hold in its body heat. A penguin also has a thick layer of blubber (fat) under its skin for insulation.

The Arctic can support a greater variety of organisms than the Antarctic because it has warmer summers. The Arctic includes the Arctic Ocean, thousands of islands, and the northernmost parts of Europe, Asia, and North America. Most Arctic organisms live on the tundra, a treeless, swampy plain.

Snowy owls live on the Arctic tundra. This owl blends perfectly with its icy habitat.

Tundra animals include birds, such as snowy owls and ptarmigan; mammals, such as polar bears, seals, lemmings, voles, snowshoe hares, and arctic foxes; and many kinds of fish. Beneath the surface of the tundra, there is a frozen layer of soil called permafrost, which never thaws. In some places, the permafrost layer may be as much as 4,510 feet (1,375 m) thick. Permafrost is the reason why trees, which need deep roots to anchor them, can't grow on the tundra. However, the tundra's top layer of soil does thaw in the summer, allowing a variety of smaller plants to grow. Many of them produce colorful flowers.

Arctic plants and animals have many adaptations that help them survive their bitterly cold habitat. Sedges and mosses grow low to the ground, which helps protect them from the whipping winds. Arctic birds and mammals stay warm because they have thick coats of feathers or fur and thick layers of blubber. And many of them spend the winter protected in burrows, caves, or dens. Fish can swim in the icy waters without turning into fishsicles because many of them make chemicals that keep their blood from freezing.

Polar bears also have many amazing cold-weather adaptations. Their bodies do a great job keeping them warm. They have thick fur, a 4-inch (10-cm) layer of blubber under their skin, and furry feet. Their fur is made up of hollow, tubelike hairs. Sunlight passes through the tubes to the polar bear's black skin, which absorbs the light instead of reflecting it, warming the bear's body. At the same time, the air trapped inside the hollow hairs keeps the heat from escaping. The hair on the bottoms of the polar bear's feet keeps them warm and allows the bear to walk on ice without slipping.

Sometimes an arctic fox will follow a polar bear so it can eat the bear's leftovers. But the fox has to stay out of sight, or the polar bear will make the fox its next meal.

Do Polar Bears Eat Penguins?

They would if they lived in the same habitat. Actually, polar bears and penguins live on opposite ends of the world! Polar bears live in the Arctic, and penguins live in the Antarctic (and other areas south of the equator).

Living on the Edge

Just 500 miles (805 km) southwest of Acapulco, Mexico, and about 1.5 miles (2.4 km) underwater, a team of researchers discovered a biological community adapted to one of the most extreme habitats on Earth. Sunlight doesn't reach this deep into the sea, so no plants can grow there. However, many living things can thrive clustered around gaps in the ocean floor called hydrothermal vents. Hydrothermal vents are like miniature underwater volcanoes. When they "erupt," they spew superheated water that kills every living thing nearby. The water from a hydrothermal vent may be more than 700°F (371°C), compared to 36°F (2°C) in the surrounding deep ocean waters. The superheated water doesn't boil because of the intense pressure at that depth.

Soon, as the area cools, new life appears around the vents. Heat is a form of energy. Bacteria living in the deep sea can use this energy and sulfur compounds in the water to make food. They gather around the vents and multiply. The bacteria, in turn, become food for sea animals such as crabs, tube worms, and mussels, which also gather around the vents. In just one year, the number of species living around a vent can double.

The artic fox (left) *has adapted to life in the Arctic. It has different adaptations from fox species in other parts of the world, such as the fennec fox* (right), *found in desert regions in Africa.*

The arctic fox is a small animal—about the size of a large house cat. It has shorter legs, a shorter snout, and smaller ears than foxes in warmer regions. These are all heat-conserving adaptations, since a smaller body means less body surface to lose heat. Like other arctic animals, the arctic fox has thick fur covering its body, including hair on the bottoms of its feet, to keep it warm and prevent slipping.

chapter four

When Seasons Change

Are there seasons where you live? No matter where on Earth you make your home, the answer is probably yes. In much of the world, there are four seasons: winter, spring, summer, and fall. As the seasons change, so do temperatures and other weather conditions. After the cold winter, the temperature gradually rises until the hot days of the summer. Then temperatures begin to fall until it is winter again. The cycle of seasons repeats itself every year. In the tropics and subtropics, there are typically two seasons—the rainy season and the dry season. These seasons are not as regular as those in the rest of the world.

All living things have ways of coping with the changing seasons. For example, some animals survive colder weather by growing thicker coats and storing fat under their skin. Some store food in their burrows, dens, or caves and hide out there all winter.

Maple trees change colors with the changing seasons. This one has green leaves in the spring and summer (top left), *no leaves in the winter* (bottom left), *and orange or red leaves in the fall* (top and bottom right).

Others leave their habitats during the winter and travel to warmer regions, where the weather is more comfortable and food is more plentiful. Plants grow very slowly—or don't grow at all—during the winter. Many of them lose their leaves and appear dead, only to come back to life in the spring.

People adapt to the seasons, too. They stay cool in the summer by using air conditioning, wearing light clothing, or going swimming. In the winter, they stay warm by heating their homes and wearing warm clothing when they go outside.

A Winter Slumber

Many animals survive cold weather and a limited food supply by sleeping. But this kind of sleep, called hibernation, isn't ordinary sleep. It is an energy-saving process that allows animals to stop eating for a long period without starving to death.

Many hibernating animals, such as bears and woodchucks, eat lots of food in the fall to get ready for winter. Their bodies store the food as fat, which provides energy for body functions during hibernation. Some hibernating animals, such as chipmunks, store food in their burrows instead of their bodies. They don't sleep straight through the winter as other hibernators do. They go through alternating

Black bears like this one hibernate through the cold winter months in North America.

periods of deep hibernation and wakefulness. When they are awake, they eat some of their stored food.

During hibernation, an animal's body processes change dramatically. The body temperature of a squirrel, for example, may drop to almost freezing while it hibernates. Its heartbeat

Are Bears True Hibernators?

Some scientists say that bears don't really hibernate. Their body temperature doesn't drop very much compared to the body temperatures of other hibernators. A bear's body temperature falls only 5° to 9°F (3° to 7°C) below its normal range of 87.8° to 99° F (31° to 37.2°C). This means bears can wake up almost instantly if danger threatens. They can also become active on warm winter days, leaving their dens for a snack.

Other scientists say that bears are true hibernators but hibernate more efficiently than small animals. Their heavy, well-insulated bodies don't lose much heat, and their stored fat supplies enough energy to run their body reactions all through the winter if necessary. A chipmunk's small body, on the other hand, can store enough energy for only a few days. Then it must warm its body enough to wake up and eat some more. After that, it cools down again. This repeated warming and cooling wastes energy.

slows from about 150 beats per minute to five beats per minute. Its breathing also slows, from about two hundred breaths per minute to four or five breaths per minute. A hibernator's metabolism (the chemical reactions that go on in its body cells) slows down greatly as well, reducing its need for food. With all its body processes running as slowly as possible, a hibernating animal doesn't wake up easily.

A Summer Snooze

Just as hibernation helps some animals survive cold seasons, another kind of inactive state called estivation helps other animals survive hot, dry seasons. Many amphibians and reptiles estivate, and so do some insects, snails, fish, and even one lemur species. Like hibernation, estivation is an energy-saving process. An estivating animal's breathing and heart rate slow down. It doesn't move, grow, or eat during this time.

To avoid drying out in the summer heat, a snail protects its moist body by hiding inside its shell. It stops moving and eating and covers its shell opening with a thin layer of mucus. As the mucus dries and hardens, it forms a plug

This banded wood snail is estivating to save energy during a dry spell in the summer.

A frog pokes its head out of the mud. During dry weather, frogs bury themselves in the mud until it rains again.

that holds moisture inside. The snail's body systems all slow down. When the dry spell ends, the snail wakes up from its summer snooze, breaks the plug, and emerges from its shell. Like snails, frogs need moisture to survive. During a drought, a frog buries itself deep in mud and estivates until it rains again.

Leaving Home

Another way animals adapt to changing seasons is by migrating (moving from one place to another). Many birds, whales, fish, insects, and turtles leave their homes and travel to different habitats when seasons change. Some migrate to escape cold weather. Some travel to different climates in search of more plentiful food. And some migrate at the same time each year to areas where they can reproduce.

Uncommon Migration

Many animals migrate from colder environments to warmer ones. But humpback whales migrate from warm tropical waters to the bitterly cold wintertime Arctic waters to eat their favorite food, krill. During the summer in the tropics, where no krill live, the whales live off their stored body fat.

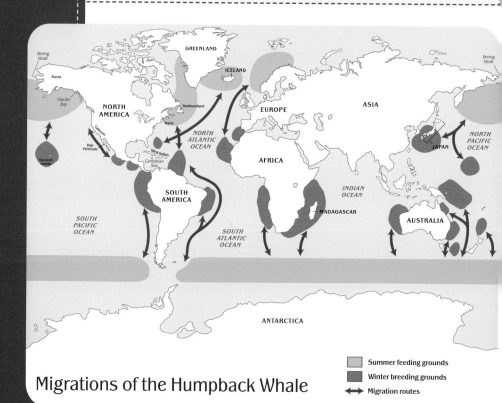

Migrations of the Humpback Whale

Summer feeding grounds
Winter breeding grounds
Migration routes

Unlike other migrators, humpback whales move to a colder habitat in the winter and a warmer habitat in the summer.

Geese fly in a V formation as they migrate south for the winter.

The comfortable temperatures and plentiful food in their breeding areas give their offspring a better start in life than they would have if the parents stayed home all year round.

Canada geese spend the spring and summer in Canada or the northern half of the United States. In the fall, as the days grow shorter, many of these birds migrate to warmer regions, traveling as far south as northern Mexico. To prepare for the long trip, the geese eat plenty of grains, grasses, insects, and plants so they can gain strength and body fat. The geese fly at 40 to 60 miles per hour (64 to 97 km per hour) and travel up to 3,000 miles (4,828 km) during the migration. Groups of geese fly together in a V formation. They take turns leading at the point of the V to break the wind resistance for the rest of the birds. In the spring, when days are getting longer again, the geese fly north to their summer homes.

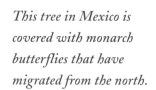

This tree in Mexico is covered with monarch butterflies that have migrated from the north.

Monarch butterflies are also amazing long-distance travelers. Every fall thousands of these black-and-orange butterflies migrate up to 2,000 miles (3,219 km) from Canada and the northern United States to California, Florida, and Mexico. Many of these butterflies don't live long enough to make the return trip home. Dangers such as storms, predators, exhaustion, and humans claim a lot of monarch lives. (Cars crush thousands of butterflies resting overnight on the warm pavement of major highways.) Monarch butterflies eat flowers to build up their fat, which supplies them with energy for their journey. They rest in huge clusters—often on tree branches—where they conserve energy by staying very still and sharing body heat. In the spring, they head back north. Along the way, the females lay eggs. Once the offspring can fly, they also head north.

"Sleeping" Plants

In the winter, it seems like much of the plant life is dead. Grass turns brown, and trees lose their leaves.

But these plants aren't dead; they're dormant. Dormancy is a kind of resting period, when plants stop growing. It helps them survive in places where the weather is too cold or dry for growth during part of the year.

For perennial plants, such as grass, dandelions, and daffodils, most growth takes place in the spring. Growth slows down during the hot, dry periods of the summer. As the weather turns colder in the fall and winter, some perennial plants may seem to die. But their roots are still alive in a dormant state. Trees also go dormant in areas with cold winters, and some of them lose all their leaves. Conifers, such as pines and firs, keep their needle-like leaves through the winter, but these trees don't grow.

Annual plants are plants that live for just one growing season. They stop growing and eventually die after they have produced their seeds. The seeds are dormant; they are alive, but they don't do anything until conditions are right for growth. Seeds can stay dormant through a winter or through a dry season. When the next growing season brings more favorable temperatures and/or rain, the seeds sprout, grow, and bear seeds of their own. Many food crops, from cucumbers and corn to tomatoes and beans, are annuals. People must plant new seeds each year to grow these foods.

Seasonal Timetables

Temperature and weather are not the only conditions that change when seasons change. Everywhere on Earth, except near the equator, the lengths of day and night change as the Earth circles the sun. In the summer, days are long and nights are short. The days shorten through autumn. The shortest days and longest nights are in the winter. In the spring, the days lengthen again.

Many plants and animals use the lengths of the day and night as cues to start various parts of their life cycle. In the spring, trees and other perennial plants burst with new green leaves, and flowers begin to open and form seeds. For animals, the lengths of day and night trigger activities such as breeding and migration. Most animals time mating so their offspring will be born when food is plentiful.

Day length is often a more reliable signal of seasonal change than temperature. For example, if plants grew new leaves and blossoms as soon as the weather turned warm, they might use up all their energy for new growth during a January thaw. The next freeze would kill all the tender new buds, and the plant would be unable to grow when spring really arrived.

Day and Night

In the northern hemisphere, the summer solstice (the longest day of the year) occurs on June 21 or 22. The winter solstice (the shortest day of the year) falls on December 21 or 22. On the spring and fall equinoxes, around March 21 and September 23, respectively, in the northern hemisphere, the hours of daylight and darkness are roughly equal. The dates are reversed in the southern hemisphere.

Perfect Timing

Tent caterpillars are the worst enemy of North American black cherry trees. Moths lay their eggs in silken tents glued to the tree branches. Hundreds of young caterpillars hatch in the spring, just in time for the opening of the first leaf buds. The wiggly caterpillars can quickly chomp their way through all the new leaves on a tree. The trees buy some help in their fight against these pests by making a sweet juice that oozes from the young leaves. Ants climb up the trees to enjoy this juicy treat, then stay to eat the caterpillars. Within a few weeks, the ants can wipe out a whole brood of tent caterpillars. The few caterpillars that survive eventually grow too big for the ants to handle. When the ants can no longer help, the trees thriftily stop making the sweet nectar. Soon no more ants come to visit.

chapter five

Adapting to the Night Life

Picture your room when it's messy: Your chair is pulled out from your desk, which is covered with books and papers. A skateboard is hiding under some clothes in the middle of the floor. Your pillow fell off the bed. You wake up before dawn, needing to use the bathroom. If you turn on the light, you'll see everything in your room clearly. Your eyes work so well that you could easily walk from the bed to the door without tripping over the mess. But what if the light bulb were burned out? Would you be able to find your way through the obstacle course in your room? Probably not.

Most animals (including humans) need light to find their way around their environments. Even in dim light, we tend to stumble and bump into things. But that's not the case for nocturnal animals. They are specially adapted to the night life. Some diurnal animals (those that are active during the day) also have adaptations to darkness because they live in dark habitats, such as

Adaptation

tunnels or murky waters, which are dark both day and night.

Animals have adapted to darkness in a variety of ways. Some have special eyes for seeing in extremely dim light. Some "see" where they're going by using their ears. Others feel their way around, and still others find their way using their senses of smell and taste.

The Eyes Have It

Hoot! Hoot! That's a familiar sound to people who spend time outdoors at night. Owls are common nocturnal birds, found in most parts of the world. They have really big eyes, as do many other nocturnal animals. Their pupils (dark openings in the centers of the eyes) are extra large to let in as much light as possible. This adaptation helps the owl see and catch its prey at night, when the only available light may come from the stars, moon, or distant street lights. Owls can't see in complete darkness, but they do see fairly well in dim light. The backs of their eyes have a layer of cells, called the tapetum, that reflects any light entering the eye. Owls can see at night about ten times better than humans can.

Owls are nocturnal animals with adaptations that help them see at night.

You've probably seen a cat's eyes glowing when light shines into them. That's the tapetum. It works the same way in cats as it does in owls, helping them catch prey in dim light—a very useful ability for nighttime hunters.

Seeing with Sounds

Even on the darkest nights, bats can snatch up tiny flying insects outdoors. They can also fly about in their crowded, pitch-black caves without bumping into anything. Despite the old saying *blind as a bat*, bats aren't blind at all. Some bat species can see very well, and all of them can see to some extent. But most bats use their ears, not their eyes, to find their way around.

If you were to blindfold any North American bat, it

Bats are nocturnal animals that use their sense of hearing to find their way around.

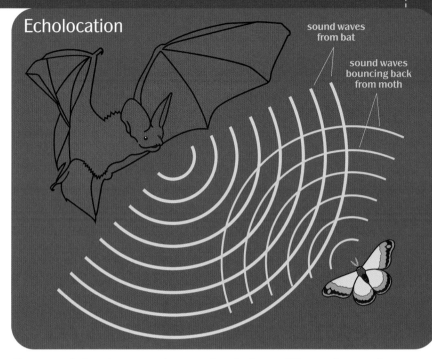

Echolocation

sound waves from bat

sound waves bouncing back from moth

Bats use echolocation to navigate and to find prey. They make sounds and listen to the returning echoes, which tell the bats about their surroundings.

could navigate perfectly. But if you plugged its ears, nose, or mouth, it would blunder around helplessly, bumping into things. That's because it must both make and hear sounds to navigate. Through its nose or mouth, the bat sends out a series of ultrasounds (sounds too high-pitched for humans to hear). If there is anything in the bat's path, the sound waves bounce off the object and return to the bat as echoes. The bat's large ears capture the echoes. Within a split second, the bat uses the echoes to figure out the shape of the object, how far away it is, and how it is moving. This navigation system is called echolocation. A bat's echolocation system is so efficient that it can locate moving prey as tiny as a mosquito and plot a flight path to catch it.

These humpback whales are using echolocation to find their way through the dark ocean.

Bats aren't the only animals that use echolocation. Dolphins and whales use echolocation to navigate through dark, murky waters. Like bats, these marine animals use sound to avoid obstacles and danger and to locate prey. Whales and dolphins make clicking sounds. Some of them are ultrasounds, and others can be heard by humans.

Feeling Their Way

If a mouse scurries across the kitchen floor in the middle of the night, a house cat doesn't need a night light to track its movements. Cats can tell a lot from the vibrations they feel through the soles of their feet. The pads on their paws and the hairs between the pads are very sensitive to touch. They are so sensitive that a cat can feel whether a mouse is coming or

Fish Whiskers

Catfish got their name because they have whiskers (called barbels) much like cats have. Their barbels help them find their way through the muddy waters they live in. But they use the sense of taste, not touch. A catfish's barbels contain special cells that taste the water to locate food. The barbels move from side to side trying to detect food.

going. Cats can also use their whiskers (long, stiff hairs on a cat's upper lip, chin, cheeks, and brow) to detect vibrations from anything moving nearby. When a cat catches a mouse, its whiskers curl around its prey to keep track of its squirming. A cat can also feel its way around a pitch-black room with its whiskers to avoid bumping into walls and other objects.

Whiskers help a cat use its sense of touch for hunting and moving around in the dark.

This mole is leaving its dark burrow.

Moles depend heavily on their sense of touch to find their way around. They live in dark burrows and spend a lot of time digging underground. A mole is almost blind, but it has thousands of sensitive cells on its hairless pink snout. These special cells can detect vibrations made by any moving object. Different types of vibrations tell the mole whether a tasty meal or possible danger lies ahead. The mole's short tail is covered with sensitive hairs. As the mole travels through its burrow, it often brushes its tail against the walls and roof to detect vibrations.

Many snakes, such as rattlesnakes, can find their prey in the dark by detecting the prey's body heat. They have heat-sensitive organs on their face, between the nose and eyes, that can detect temperature differences as tiny as a thousandth of a

A rattlesnake has no trouble finding prey in the dark. It can detect heat from other animals both day and night.

degree. A snake's heat sensors help its brain form a fuzzy image of the prey so the snake can locate it even in the dark.

The Nose Knows

Sharks can navigate cloudy ocean waters by using their sense of smell. A shark smells through two nostrils on the underside of its snout. It doesn't breathe through its nostrils as land animals do. Sharks use their nostrils for only one purpose: to find food.

A great white shark like this one uses its very sensitive nose to find food.

A shark's sense of smell is so effective that it can locate one drop of blood in 25 gallons (95 liters) of water—the amount it takes to fill a small wading pool. It can smell its prey from 0.25 mile (0.4 km) away.

A shark relies mostly on its keen sense of smell to find prey, but this sense works best in combination with the shark's other senses. Sharks have keen hearing too, and many have good eyesight. They also use their sense of touch to feel nearby movement in the water. They can even detect electrical fields created by prey.

Cavefish

Imagine living in a cave, where it's pitch-black day and night. You have no use for your eyes because there's no light. You have to rely on your other senses to get around without bumping into things. Now imagine that this cave is underwater.

Cavefish live in underwater caves in lakes and streams in the southern United States and in Mexico, Central America, and South America. They have eyes when they are very young, but they don't use them. It's too dark in their caves to see anything. As the fish grow, their eyes disappear.

Adult cavefish, like the ones shown above, have no eyes. These fish live in pitch-black underwater caves.

Adult cavefish have no eyes at all. They're completely blind, but they can find their way around quite well. They locate food with an amazing sense of smell. They also have sense organs along their sides (lateral lines) that are highly sensitive to vibrations. These vibrations help them avoid bumping into things in the water.

Scientists have conducted experiments on cavefish to see if the fish could grow new eyes. When scientists transplanted eye lenses from other fish into the cavefish, these blind fish started to grow eyes. Scientists hope that this discovery may someday help doctors treat blind people.

chapter six

Prey versus Predator

In a community of life, each organism eats other organisms, gets eaten, or both. Plants are food for many animals. Many animals are food (prey) for hunting animals (predators). These interactions are nature's way of keeping a healthy balance in the community.

If predators kill all the prey in their community, it's bad news not only for the prey animals, but also for the predators. They won't have any food to eat in the future. Such an imbalance does not usually occur because many prey animal species have developed effective ways of escaping their enemies. Even plants have special adaptations that protect them from hungry animals. Predators, in turn, have their own adaptations that make them better hunters or food gatherers.

Built for Speed

Some creatures survive mainly because they are good at running, jumping, swimming, or flying away from their enemies. Deer and antelope, for example, are very fast runners. They can sprint up to 40 miles per

(Above) *Cheetahs can run faster than Thomson's gazelles. But the gazelles can outlast cheetahs in long chases and can make turns more speedily.* (Right) *This eagle is about to swoop in and catch a fish from the water.*

hour (64 km per hour). Many fish and birds are also built for speed.

Often speed alone is not enough. Some predators can run even faster than their swift prey. For example, scientists have clocked cheetahs running as fast as 70 miles per hour (113 km per hour)—much faster than the antelopes and other prey they hunt. Whales and sharks can swim 25 miles per hour (40 km per hour), more than twice as fast as minnows, bass, and other small fish. Eagles and falcons can fly more than 100 miles per hour (161 km per hour).

This rabbit is running in a zigzag pattern to escape a hungry lynx.

So an animal that tries to survive by fleeing may need more than speed. Some prey animals are not only speedy but also tricky. They dodge and dart as they flee. A rabbit chased by a fox zigzags to confuse the fox. A minnow zigzags to escape the jaws of a larger fish.

Some animals, such as fleas, frogs, and kangaroos, can escape their enemies by leaping high and fast into the air. These animals have special adaptations for jumping. Their hind legs are much longer and stronger than their forelegs.

Adaptation

Leaping Animals

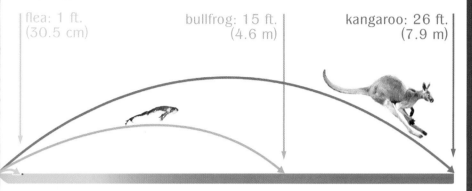

flea: 1 ft.
(30.5 cm)

bullfrog: 15 ft.
(4.6 m)

kangaroo: 26 ft.
(7.9 m)

Fleas, frogs, and kangaroos all escape their enemies by leaping.

Leaping for Their Lives

A kangaroo can cover 26 feet (7.9 m) in a single leap. That's about five times its height. A bullfrog can jump about 15 feet (4.6 m)—roughly thirty times its body length. A tiny flea can leap 1 foot (30.5 cm) into the air. That may not sound like much, but it's two hundred times a flea's body length!

Hiding Out

Some prey animals use hiding places to escape from predators. A rabbit or a prairie dog will dive into a burrow for safety. Mice and other small rodents may use tall grass for shelter. Some predators can use the same kind of trick, however. For example, a mountain lion may hide in tall grasses until its prey comes near. It slinks through the grass unseen, ready to pounce. Before the prey knows what is happening, it is too late.

A turtle can pull its head, legs, and tail inside its hard shell to protect the soft parts of its body from predators.

Some animals have a built-in hiding place. For example, two hard shells cover a turtle's body like a suit of armor. Normally the turtle's head, legs, and tail stick out between the upper and lower shells. But when danger threatens, the turtle pulls its head, legs, and tail inside the shell. Most predators give up and walk away.

If a hedgehog gets nervous or scared, it curls its body into a little ball. This position makes the hedgehog's sharp spines stand straight out in all

This hedgehog has curled into a ball to avoid danger.

directions. When the hedgehog does this, it becomes painful to touch, and many predators avoid it.

Other animals with suits of armor are bivalves, such as clams, oysters, and scallops. A bivalve has two shells connected by a very powerful muscle. It can snap its shells together and keep them closed so tightly that even a strong human can't pull them open.

Shell-Shocked

Some predators do manage to eat bivalves. A sea star uses suction cups under its arms to pull open a bivalve's shells. As soon as there is a small gap between the shells, the sea star turns its stomach inside out and slips it through the gap. It digests the bivalve right inside the shells, then pulls its stomach back into its own body.

The oystercatcher is a bird with a long, slim beak. It slips its beak between an oyster's shells when they are open. Then, using its beak like a pair of scissors, the bird quickly cuts the oyster's muscle so the oyster can't snap its shells shut.

The sea otter also eats bivalves. This mammal uses a tool, such as a flat rock, to open up oysters or clams. Floating on its back in the water, the sea otter places the rock on its belly. It cracks a bivalve's shells by hitting the rock with the bivalve.

This lion blends into the grass as it waits to pounce on a zebra.

Blending In

Many animals hide from predators or hunt prey more
effectively by using a common adaptation called
camouflage. These animals have fur, feathers, or skin
that match their habitat. For example, many desert
animals are light brown or tan. This coloring helps
them blend into a sandy or rocky landscape. The
stripes of a zebra or a tiger make it harder to spot in
tall grass. The spots of a fawn or a leopard blend with
the spotted pattern of light and shadows formed by
sunlight shining through a leafy tree.

In the Arctic, many animals change color when
the seasons change the color of their habitat. For

example, a bird called the ptarmigan has brown, earthy plumage in the summer. But in the winter, the ptarmigan's feathers are white so it can hide unnoticed in the snow. The arctic fox also changes color each season. In the summer, the fox's coat is brownish gray, but in the winter, it becomes white. In a snowy landscape, the fox's white fur helps it sneak up on prey.

Many insects and spiders use camouflage too. Stick insects look like twigs. Leaf insects look like tree leaves. Moths and butterflies resting on trees look like bark or old leaves. A crab spider can change its color to match the flower it is sitting on. If the flower is yellow, the spider is yellow, too. This disguise serves the spider as both prey and predator.

This crab spider has changed color to match the flower petal it's sitting on. The spider's camouflage not only protects it from predators but also hides it as it waits for tasty insects to happen by.

The behavior of animals with camouflage makes this adaptation even more effective. Camouflaged animals usually spend a lot of time staying still. For example, a green grasshopper is very hard to spot among blades of green grass until it hops. A fawn "freezes," curled up in a shady spot, while the mother deer is away feeding on grass or shrubs.

Color-Changing Champion

Chameleons are the camouflage champs. They can change to a wide range of striking colors: pale green, bright green, yellow, orange, red, black, and sometimes blue. A chameleon's color changes may help it blend into its surroundings, but it often changes color for other reasons, too: regulating body temperature, responding to light and darkness, reflecting a state of mind, or attracting a mate.

This chameleon has changed to match the leaf. Chameleons can turn many colors to match their surroundings.

A Diet of Poison

Brightly colored frogs in the rain forests of South and Central America are hopping advertisements. Their colors say, "Don't eat me—I'm poisonous!" Species like the poison dart frogs of Colombia make their own deadly poison. But other tropical frogs start out as shy, defenseless creatures. They gain a chemical weapon by eating ants, which use poisons called alkaloids to defend themselves and capture prey. The frogs store the ant alkaloids in special glands in their skin, where the poisons don't harm the frogs. The more ants the frogs eat, the more poisonous they become. Scientists found that ants make up nearly three-quarters of the diet of some frogs. These frogs may eat hundreds of ants each day.

Chemical Weapons

Some insects use chemical weapons to protect themselves. These insects often have bright colors, bold patterns, or bad smells. Tiger moths, monarch butterflies, and ladybugs use all three methods to advertise their poisons. Their bodies are covered with bad-tasting chemicals that can make predators sick or even kill them. Animals quickly learn that species with such colors, patterns, and smells are not good to eat.

Millipedes don't advertise their poisons, but these creatures certainly use them. Different kinds of millipedes make different chemicals to use against their enemies. Some millipedes produce camphor, the same chemical that people use in mothballs and other insect repellents. Other millipedes produce a substance that makes attackers fall asleep when they eat it. This adaptation doesn't save the victim, but it helps the victim's neighbors. Still other millipedes produce tiny amounts of poison gases. These help keep away small predators, such as fire ants. Some tropical millipedes can spray smelly chemicals at larger animals, such as birds, mammals, or lizards, up to 5 feet (1.5 m) away!

Skunks are well known for their chemical weapons. A skunk's black and white fur usually warns predators to stay away. But if another animal threatens the skunk, it doesn't need to run. Instead, it lifts its tail, aims its rear end at the predator, and sprays a terrible-smelling chemical, which lingers long after the skunk is gone. It usually takes only one skunk encounter for a predator to learn to leave skunks alone.

Some creatures use mimicry to fool their enemies. The mimics are harmless animals that resemble creatures a predator finds dangerous. For example, two kinds of orange-and-black

This skunk has raised its tail to spray an enemy with a bad-smelling chemical.

butterflies taste so bad that no bird wants to eat them. Many other orange-and-black butterflies don't taste bad. Birds usually leave all orange-and-black butterflies alone because they can't tell the difference between the tasty ones and the bad-tasting ones. Swallowtail butterfly caterpillars also use mimicry to survive, but they imitate poisonous snakes. This caterpillar has two eye spots on its rear, which makes it look like a snake's head. It tries to scare off predators by waving this "head" back and forth as if it were a snake about to strike.

This viceroy butterfly (top) *mimics the coloring of the bad-tasting monarch butterfly* (bottom). *In areas where there aren't many monarchs, viceroys resemble other kinds of bad-tasting butterflies, such as queen butterflies.*

Plant Defenses

Plants may not be able to run and hide from their enemies as many animals can, but they aren't defenseless. For example, the sharp thorns on rose stems and the prickly spines on cacti defend these plants quite effectively. Many conifers, such as spruce and pine trees, have needle-like leaves that most animals don't like to eat. The stinging nettle plant has leaves that are covered with syringe-like hairs. If an animal touches the leaves,

Let Them Be

Leaves in three, let them be is a good saying to follow if you want to avoid irritating plants like poison ivy or poison oak. These plants with three-leaf clusters contain an allergy-causing chemical that causes an itchy, burning skin rash when allergic people touch them. Poison sumac has seven to thirteen leaflets, and it is just as irritating as poison ivy and poison oak. Most people are allergic to these plants, but they don't irritate many animals—probably because fur, feathers, or scales protect the skin of most animals. People can pick up and react to the irritating chemical after touching an animal that has brushed against poison ivy, oak, or sumac.

the hairs break off and inject chemicals into the skin, causing severe irritation and swelling.

Many plants contain bad-tasting chemicals that discourage hungry animals from eating them. For example, buttercups produce shiny yellow flowers that look like tasty treats for plant-eating animals. But cattle and horses rarely eat buttercups. The animals know from experience that buttercups aren't tasty at all. They contain a very bitter juice and can even be poisonous in large amounts.

Poinsettias are plants with red leaves that many

people use as decorations at Christmastime. These plants are pretty, but they contain a bitter-tasting chemical that can make any creature that eats them very sick. Fortunately, poinsettia leaves taste so bad that few animals ever take more than one bite.

A bleeding heart plant has tall flowering stems and fern-like leaves. It produces pinkish-purple heart-shaped flowers. This lovely plant is great for gardens because it can defend itself from nibbling animals. Its stem and leaves contain a poison that is dangerous to animals that eat them.

Some plants are predators themselves. They form traps to catch insects and other small animals, on which the plants feed. For example, the Venus flytrap plant has two-part hinged leaves. Each leaf has trigger hairs that stiffen when touched by an insect. When two hairs are touched (or one is touched twice), the two leaf halves snap shut and trap the insect. The leaf stays tightly closed until the plant finishes digesting its prey.

chapter seven

Human Adaptations

Humans can live almost anywhere on Earth—even in Antarctica. Although no one really lives in Antarctica permanently, the average human population there is about 3,500 people in the summer and about 1,500 people in the winter. Most of those people are scientists doing research. They live on forty bases, where they have food, shelter, plenty of warm clothing, and anything else they need to survive in Antarctica's cold, harsh conditions.

Unlike most animals, which can survive in only one or two habitats, people can survive in a variety of conditions. Our bodies have a very useful adaptation: the ability to adjust to many different habitats. Our brains do some of the adjustment work, helping us figure out how to be comfortable in a particular environment. Our bodies do the rest of the work, changing their processes slightly so they can operate efficiently in a new environment. For example, if you live in frigid northern Alaska, and your family decides to move to steamy Florida, your body will adjust to the new climate over time. At first, when Florida temperatures fall to 60°F (16°C), you'll want to run around in shorts and a T-shirt. Your neighbors, wearing heavy jackets, will probably look at you strangely. But eventually your body will adjust to the Florida climate, and you'll react to temperatures as though you were a native.

Some human populations also have distinct physical adaptations to their environments. For example, different groups of people have inherited traits that help them survive strong sunlight, extreme heat or cold, and high altitude. And all humans have an adaptation that enables us to eat a wide-ranging diet.

Sun and Skin

People who live in similar parts of the world tend to have similar skin color. For example, the natives of countries around the equator (such as Kenya in Africa, Ecuador in South America, and Indonesia in Asia) usually have dark skin. The natives of Norway, Sweden, Iceland, and other countries in the far north usually have light skin.

> **Did You Know?**
> Freckles are spots of skin cells that contain more melanin than the rest of the skin. When a freckle-prone person exposes his or her skin to the sun, more freckles appear, and the existing freckles get darker.

The dark skin of people in the tropics is due to a dark pigment called melanin. Dark skin contains more melanin than light skin. Melanin protects the skin from the sun's

This young man has spent too much time in the sun and has sunburned his face and arms.

harmful radiation, which can cause sunburn or even skin cancer. Near the equator, the sun is very bright and hot. Dark skin is an adaptation to the conditions there.

Scientists believe that the human species first evolved in equatorial Africa. Humans had lost the dark fur coat of their apelike ancestors, but they still had dark skin, which protected them from the strong sun. Gradually humans spread to other parts of the world.

In cooler climates farther north and south of the equator, dark-skinned people have a disadvantage. Vitamin D, an important vitamin that helps build bones and keep them strong, is made in the skin when it is exposed to sunlight. Under the bright equatorial sun, enough sunlight gets through a dark-skinned person's melanin "shield" to make the necessary vitamin D. But the sunlight isn't as strong outside the tropics, so people cover much of their skin with clothing to keep warm. Dark-skinned people may not make enough vitamin D to keep their bones strong. Their bones may bend and break easily.

So the descendants of early humans who migrated to cooler climates developed a different adaptation to survive in weaker sunlight: lighter skin. Over many generations, mutations causing the skin to produce less melanin appeared and spread through the population via natural selection. Scientists think this process took about ten thousand years.

A Kind of Camouflage

Melanin, the same chemical that makes people's skin dark, also helps chameleons and other animals change color. Dark skin may have camouflaged early humans in addition to protecting them from the powerful equatorial sun. Dark coloring helps animals survive by making them harder to see. So, back in the days before people wore clothes, dark skin may have protected humans from big predators such as lions. It may also have masked them while they were hunting.

What happens if a light-skinned person visits or moves to a place where the sun is very hot and bright? Most people have some ability to adjust to this kind of change. When we expose our skin to more sunlight, our skin makes more melanin, and we gradually get a suntan. (But light-skinned people don't usually get as dark as naturally dark-skinned people.) People can also use sunscreen or light-colored clothing to protect their skin from sun damage.

Heat and Cold

Differences in skin color aren't the only ways humans have adapted to different climates. For example, people living in the tropics typically have a larger body surface per pound (kilogram) of body weight than people living in colder climates. One of the main ways living things get rid of excess heat is by transferring it from the body surface to the environment. Sweating (releasing water through tiny openings in the skin) is another way some animals (including humans) keep their bodies cool. As the sweat evaporates (becomes water vapor in the air), it takes heat with it. Animals that don't sweat, such as dogs, get rid of excess heat by panting. But both sweating and panting make animals lose precious water. People who are adapted to hot climates usually have very efficient cooling systems. Their relatively large body surface helps them transfer more heat to the environment without sweating than the bodies of people who aren't adapted to hot climates.

People in cold climates have different adaptations. For example, the Inuit (formerly known as Eskimo) of Alaska and northern Canada have more effective circulation of blood to their hands and feet than people from warmer climates. This allows them to transfer body heat to their hands and feet when they are cold. People without this adaptation may get frozen fingers and toes when they are exposed to extreme cold. The traditional Inuit diet helps make this adaptation even more effective. It

The members of this Inuit family sit in an igloo in northern Canada. Their bodies are adapted to their cold climate, but they also need to wear heavy jackets and fur-lined boots.

includes a lot of fatty fish, such as salmon, mackerel, tuna, and sardines. This high-calorie diet provides fuel for producing extra body heat. The fish oils also improve blood circulation.

Humans in general have only a limited ability to adjust to heat and cold. They can survive under more extreme conditions by using artificial aids, such as heavy clothing and electric blankets.

Getting Enough Oxygen

When the Earth first formed, its atmosphere contained no oxygen. The earliest organisms didn't need to breathe oxygen.

Instead, they used different chemical reactions to get energy. When the first plantlike organisms began using photosynthesis to make food and generate energy, they released small amounts of oxygen gas. Over millions of years, as the plantlike organisms multiplied, the amount of oxygen in the atmosphere increased. The other living things on Earth had to adapt or die. Oxygen was a poison to some of them, but others developed ways of using it. Soon this gas became necessary for nearly all the Earth's organisms.

The Earth's atmosphere contains about 21 percent oxygen up to about 60 miles (97 km) above sea level. That's far higher than Earth's tallest mountain, and it's also higher than most airplanes fly. But the atmosphere gets thinner (there is less atmosphere overall) at higher and higher altitudes. So the higher you go, the less oxygen you take in with each breath.

Human populations that have lived at high altitudes for a very long time are adapted to breathing air with less oxygen. The chests of these mountain dwellers are larger than usual, providing them with greater lung capacity, and their blood contains a higher than usual concentration of red blood cells, which can carry a great deal of oxygen.

Visitors to high-altitude areas, such as Denver,

Adaptation

Colorado (5,280 feet or about 1,609 m above sea level), or
Bogotá, Colombia (about 8,661 feet or 2,640 m), feel short of
breath. Mountain climbers often need to carry oxygen tanks.
Yet natives of Lhasa, Tibet, live at 11,975 feet (3,650 m).
Natives of the Andes live even higher: up to 16,500 feet
(5,029 m) above sea level. And the Sherpa guides of Nepal
don't need to breathe bottled oxygen even when they climb to
the peak of Mount Everest—nearly 29,028 feet (8,848 m)
above sea level.

These Sherpa men from Nepal train in the mountains to guide tourists
up Mount Everest. Sherpas are famous for their mountaineering skills,
as well as for their physical adaptations to high altitude.

Unfair Olympics?

The 1968 Olympics took place in Mexico City, 7,349 feet (2,240 m) above sea level. Athletes from countries close to sea level complained that they had an unfair disadvantage because they weren't allowed to train at high altitude before the games. After a few weeks at high altitude, the number of oxygen-carrying red blood cells in human blood nearly doubles—but the athletes had only about two weeks in Mexico City. Athletes from high-altitude countries could, of course, train at home—and they had a lifelong adjustment to low oxygen levels.

Airplanes can fly above the highest mountains. Their pressurized cabins can hold air that's more highly concentrated than the atmosphere where they fly. An airplane carries oxygen masks in case damage to the plane causes it to lose air pressure. These masks are vital for safety. At 5,000 feet (1,524 m), a pilot in an unpressurized aircraft becomes less able to make quick decisions. At higher altitudes, the pilot may lose consciousness.

Astronauts fly beyond the Earth's atmosphere, where there is no oxygen at all. Spacecrafts, like airplanes, are pressurized and carry their own air

Humans can climb or fly to very high altitudes. But people usually need either time to adjust to thin atmosphere or tools that provide the oxygen they need to survive.

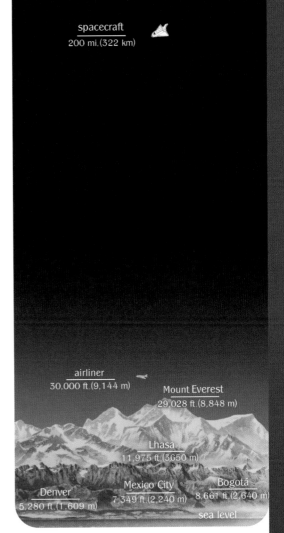

Altitude Comparison

spacecraft
200 mi.(322 km)

airliner
30,000 ft.(9,144 m)

Mount Everest
29,028 ft.(8,848 m)

Lhasa
11,975 ft.(3650 m)

Mexico City
7,349 ft.(2,240 m)

Bogotá
8,661 ft.(2,640 m)

Denver
5,280 ft.(1,609 m)

sea level

supply. When an astronaut makes repairs outside a spacecraft, he or she wears a pressurized suit. The astronaut uses an air lock (a small chamber with one tight-sealing door leading inside the spacecraft and another leading outside) to keep the craft's air from escaping.

You Are What You Eat

You can tell a lot about what a mammal eats by looking at its teeth. Some mammals are carnivores, which eat mainly meat. Others are herbivores, which eat mainly plants. Still others are omnivores, which eat both meat and plants.

Carnivores, like this cougar, have sharp canine teeth for stabbing and holding their prey.

Carnivores, such as cats and dogs, have four long, pointed canine teeth. The canines serve as knives for stabbing and holding prey. Their back teeth are also pointed for tearing up food and grinding bones. A carnivore's front teeth are relatively small. Carnivores don't use their front teeth much in eating. In fact, these animals don't really chew their food. They bite it into chunks and swallow the chunks whole.

Herbivores, such as horses and rabbits, have large, well-developed front teeth (incisors). These teeth are wide and flat, with sharp edges. Herbivores use them like scissors, to snip off plant leaves and stems or to bite chunks out of roots and fruits. (Some herbivores, such as sheep, cattle, and goats, have a bony plate instead of upper incisors.) An herbivore's back teeth

(Above) *Horses are herbivores. They have wide, flat, sharp front teeth that are good for eating plants.* (Below) *Humans are omnivores. Our teeth are a variety of shapes and sizes to manage the many different foods we eat.*

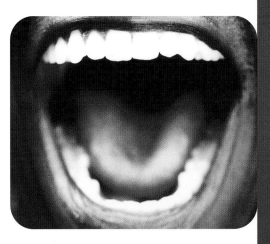

are large and broad for grinding grains and other plant matter. Herbivores have no canines—just a gap between the front and back teeth.

Omnivores have a complete set of teeth for eating all kinds of foods. Like herbivores, they have incisors for cutting and broad back teeth for grinding. Their canines aren't as large as those of carnivores, but they are sharp and useful for tearing food. This all-purpose set of teeth should seem familiar. You see one like it in the mirror every day, for you are an omnivore.

Specialized teeth are not humans' only dietary adaptation. Our digestive system suits our diet too. Plant foods are rather hard to digest, so herbivores usually have long intestines to allow plenty of digesting time. Some herbivores, such as cows, even have extra stomachs to help break down the food. They may also regurgitate (burp up) partly digested food so they can chew it again. Meat is much easier to digest than plant foods, so carnivores typically have much shorter intestines than herbivores have. Omnivores usually have medium-length intestines to cope with their mixed diet.

As an omnivore, you have a big advantage over more specialized eaters. If one kind of food is scarce, you can get along on whatever other food is available. Having a diet that's too specialized can threaten an animal's survival. For example, the koalas of Australia eat mainly the leaves and shoots of eucalyptus trees. Koalas in the wild rarely drink water; they get the water they need from eucalyptus leaves. If a disaster destroyed the eucalyptus trees, many koalas would die.

This koala bear is sitting in a eucalyptus tree. A koala's diet is made up almost entirely of eucalyptus leaves.

Humans have been our planet's biggest success story so far, mainly because we are able to adjust to different conditions so easily. We're not very specialized. We can't run as fast as a deer or a cheetah; we don't have big fangs like a tiger; we can't live underwater like a fish. But we have one big advantage over all other living things: our brain. We can think our way out of all kinds of problems, from finding food to escaping enemies to exploring new habitats. If we can't adjust physically to a change in conditions, we can make and use artificial devices. For example, scuba gear lets us swim underwater, heated buildings allow us to live in cold climates, and shipping enables us to eat foods that don't grow naturally in our local habitats. Perhaps someday we'll even use our abilities to travel to other planets and make new homes there.

Glossary

adaptation: a change in a species that makes it more fit for survival in a particular environment

adaptive radiation: a process in which two or more species evolve from a common ancestor and then become increasingly different over time; divergent evolution

amphibian: an organism that can live both in the water and on land. Amphibians include frogs, toads, salamanders, and caecilians.

analogous structures: body parts in different species that look similar and serve similar needs but differ in structure. Analogous body parts evolved in different ways from different ancestors.

annual plants: plants that complete their life cycle in one growing season

Antarctica: the continent surrounding the South Pole

Arctic: the region surrounding the North Pole

blubber: a layer of fat underneath the skin

camouflage: an organism's color, pattern, or shape that blends in with its surroundings, making the organism less noticeable

canopy: the level of a forest habitat formed by the trees' leafy upper branches

carnivore: an animal that eats mainly meat

cartilage: a tough, stretchy tissue in all vertebrates and some invertebrates. Shark skeletons are all cartilage. Adult human skeletons contain small amounts of cartilage, generally at the ends of bones.

convergent evolution: a process in which distantly related species independently develop similar adaptations

deoxyribonucleic acid (DNA): a molecule that contains, in chemical code, all the instructions a cell needs to live. These instructions pass from parent to offspring when organisms reproduce.

diurnal: active during the day

divergent evolution: a process in which two or more species evolve from a common ancestor and then become increasingly different over time; adaptive radiation

dormant: temporarily inactive; in a resting state

echolocation: a navigation system in which an animal (such as a bat or a dolphin) sends out sounds that bounce off objects and echo back to the animal's ears. The animal uses the echoes to figure out an object's shape, distance, and movement.

emergent layer: the highest level of a rain forest, made up of the tops of the tallest trees rising above the canopy

equinox: a day in spring or fall when the hours of daylight and darkness are roughly equal

estivation: temporary inactive state for surviving hot or dry conditions

evolution: the process by which species change over time as they adapt to Earth's conditions

extinction: the death of all members of a species

genes: chemical units that make up DNA. Each gene influences one or more hereditary traits.

habitat: the environment where an organism naturally lives

herbivore: an animal that eats mainly plants

hibernation: a temporary inactive state for surviving cold conditions

homologous structures: body parts in different species that have the same basic structure (suggesting a common origin) but very different forms (often for different uses)

humidity: water vapor in the air

hydrothermal vent: a crack in the ocean floor that spews superheated water (up to 700°F or 371°C)

invertebrate: animal without a backbone

melanin: dark pigment in an animal's skin or hair

metabolism: all the chemical reactions that go on in an organism's body

migration: moving from one location to another to find more plentiful food or water, or a more suitable climate, or to reproduce

mimicry: resemblance by a harmless animal to a creature that a predator finds dangerous

mutation: a DNA change caused by a copying error during cell division. Mutations may cause changes in body structures or functions.

natural selection: a process in which organisms compete for survival, and those best suited to their environments survive and reproduce; "survival of the fittest"

niche: an organism's role in its community of life

nocturnal: active at night

omnivore: an animal that eats both meat and plants

perennial plants: plants that survive for three growing seasons or more

permafrost: a permanently frozen layer of soil

photosynthesis: a process in which organisms use sunlight energy to make sugar from carbon dioxide and water, producing oxygen as a by-product

physical adaptation: a change in the structure of an organism (such as a change in a leg or beak) that makes the organism better fit for survival in its environment

predator: an animal that hunts, kills, and eats other animals

prey: an animal that's killed and eaten by other animals

solstice: the longest or shortest day of the year

species: a group of organisms that share many hereditary traits and (usually) can breed only with one another

tapetum: a reflective layer of cells at the backs of the eyes of some nocturnal animals. The tapetum helps an animal see in dim light.

tundra: in the Arctic, a cold, treeless, swampy plain

understory: the level of a rain forest between the canopy and the ground. It consists of small trees, vines, and palms, as well as shrubs and ferns.

variations: differences within a single trait (such as hair color) for a species that pass from parent to offspring during reproduction

vertebrate: an animal with a backbone

Selected Bibliography

Audesirk, Theresa, and Gerald Audesirk. *Biology: Life on Earth.* 4th ed. Upper Saddle River, NJ: Prentice-Hall, 1996.

Capon, Brian. *Plant Survival: Adapting to a Hostile World.* Portland, OR: Timber Press, 1994.

Glass, Susan. *Adaptation and Survival.* Logan, IA: Perfection Learning Corporation, 2005.

Hoagland, Mahlon, and Bert Dodson. *The Way Life Works.* New York: Times Books, 1995.

Kalman, Bobbie. *How Do Animals Adapt?* New York: Crabtree Publishing Company, 2000.

Parker, Steve. *Adaptation.* Chicago: Heinemann Library, 2001.

Silverstein, Alvin, Virginia B. Silverstein, and Laura Silverstein Nunn. *Evolution.* Minneapolis, MN: Millbrook Press, 1998.

Winkler, Peter. *Animal Adaptations.* Washington, DC: National Geographic Society, 2004.

For Further Information

Books

Fleisher, Paul. *Evolution*. Minneapolis, MN: Twenty-First Century Books, 2006.

Goodman, Susan E. *Claws, Coats, and Camouflage: The Ways Animals Fit into Their World*. Minneapolis: Millbrook Press, 2001.

Stewart, Melissa. *Life in a Wetland*, Ecosystems in Action series. Minneapolis: Twenty-First Century Books, 2003.

Tagliaferro, Linda. *Galápagos Island: Nature's Delicate Balance at Risk*. Minneapolis: Twenty-First Century Books, 2001.

Townsend, John. *Would You Survive? Animal and Plant Adaptation*. Chicago: Raintree Fusion, 2006.

———. *Would You Survive? Living Things in Habitats*. Chicago: Raintree Fusion, 2006.

VanCleave, Janice. *Science around the World: Activities on Biomes from Pole to Pole*. Hoboken, NJ: John Wiley & Sons, 2004.

Vogt, Gregory L. *The Biosphere: Realm of Life*. Minneapolis: Twenty-First Century Books, 2007.

Websites

Animal Adaptations
> http://www.widgeon.com/Wilson/Grade4/SelectedAnimals.html. This site offers facts about more than thirty animals and their adaptations for survival, plus pictures of dozens of animals to color online.

Animal Adaptations and Survival
> http://www.woodlands-junior.kent.sch.uk/Homework/adaptation.htm. This science homework help site provides facts, questions, and answers about adaptations to various habitats.

Animal Adaptations Pathfinder
   http://www.itss.brockport.edu/~llac0731/605.html. This site provides links to many websites about adaptations, plus links to fun animal games.

Animals on Defense
   http://oncampus.richmond.edu/academics/education/projects/webunits /adaptations. This site, created by students at the University of Richmond, offers fun activities and information on animal adaptations such as camouflage, hibernation, migration, and mimicry.

Earth Floor
   http://www.cotf.edu/ete/modules/msese/earthsysflr/adapt .html. This website's "elevator" transports users to facts about adaptation and related topics such as diversity, cycles, and biomes.

EcoKids
   http://www.ecokidsonline.com/pub/index.cfm. This lively site provides games, activities, calendars, screen savers, and information about science, nature, and environmental issues.

Habitats/Biomes
   http://www.enchantedlearning.com/biomes. This colorful site contains information on Earth's varied habitats and the animals that live there, as well as printouts and monthly activity calendars.

Plant Adaptations
   http://www.mbgnet.net/bioplants/adapt.html. At this website, users can learn how plants have adapted for survival in various biomes: desert, grassland, tropical rain forest, temperate rain forest, temperate deciduous forest, taiga, tundra, and in water. Users can also play an adaptation game and sing an adaptation song.

World Biomes
   http://www.blueplanetbiomes.org/world_biomes.htm. This site is full of facts about Earth's biomes, including tundra, taiga, grassland, deciduous forest, chaparral, desert, desert-scrub, savanna, rain forest, and alpine.

Index

Photo Acknowledgments

About the Authors

Dr. Alvin Silverstein is a former professor of biology and director of the Physician Assistant Program at the College of Staten Island of the City University of New York.

Virginia B. Silverstein is a translator of Russian scientific literature. The Silversteins' collaboration began with a biochemical research project at the University of Pennsylvania. Since then they have produced six children and more than two hundred published books that have received high acclaim for their clear, timely, and authoritative coverage of science and health topics.

Laura Silverstein Nunn, a graduate of Kean College, began helping with the research for her parents' books while she was in high school. Since joining the writing team, she has coauthored more than eighty books.